Noah

Elephant

NOAH AND THE ARK

Illustrated by Chris Rothero

It's fun to Read Along

Here's what you do –

These pictures are some of the characters and things the story tells about. Let the child to whom you are reading SEE and SAY them.

Then, as you read the story text and come to a picture instead of a word, pause and point to the picture for your listener to SEE and SAY.

You'll be amazed at how quickly children catch on and enjoy participating in the story telling.

Ark

Raven

Dove

Window

ISBN 1-84135-036-2

Copyright © 1994 Award Publications Limited

First published 1994
This edition first published 2000

Published by Award Publications Limited,
1st Floor, 27 Longford Street, London NW1 3DZ

Printed in Belgium

Mountains

Hippos

Rainbow

Animals

Lioness

Trees

NOAH AND THE ARK

There was once a very old man

called  . One day God

talked to  . He told him to

build a special kind of boat called

an  . God told  exactly

how to build his .

 's three sons helped him

to build the  , and when it
was finished it had a  and a
 just as God commanded.

There was also room for all the

different  and

 was told to take on board.

"In seven days," God told

 , "there will be a great

flood but you and the animals will

be safe."

If you have ever had a  's  you will know some of the animals that floated away on her.

There would be an and his mate, and two fat heavy and most likely a  and  not to mention two , and maybe two !

Every living thing that could

walk or creep or fly  took

into his  . And among the

birds were the big strong-flying

 and the gentle little white-

winged . They were useful

to  when the time came to

leave the  .

When saw that all the  were in the , he took his family aboard and shut the

. In seven days down came the rain. And how it rained! It rained and rained until all the land was covered with water.

The rose higher and

higher in the flood. Soon the tops

of the were covered.

The  bobbed about like a

cork and inside  and his

family were perfectly dry.

The rains stopped at last and

's wonderful  came to

rest on top of a mountain. When

 thought it was safe, he sent out his . When it did not return,  knew it had found a resting place.

 sent out his pretty white  after the but she was soon back and he opened the  of the  to let her in.

The  had failed to find a

leafy  on which to perch.

But when  sent her out again, the returned with a green in her mouth. This told the were no

longer under water.

A third time  opened the window of his and sent out

his and this time she did not

return. "The water covering the

earth has dried up,"  told his

family. "The 🕊 has not come

back to the ."

And  opened the

and stepped on to dry land.

Then  and his three sons

set free all the beasts and birds,

and none had come to harm in the

 . And out came the s

and the  and and so

many other kinds of beasts and

birds that  had no names for.

 was grateful to God for

having saved him and his family

from the flood.

"Let us remember this place,"

 said to his sons as they

stood by the watching the

last of the big  fly away into

the sky. God was pleased with

 because  had

remembered him.

"I will set a  in the

heavens, which will be a sign to

you that never again will there

be such a flood ..."

 looked up into the sky

and saw the  and his old

heart was at peace.